tECHiES™

Jeff Bezos

Jeff Bezos

{ King of Amazon }

JOSEPHA SHERMAN

TWENTY-FIRST CENTURY BOOKS

BROOKFIELD, CONNECTICUT

Special thanks to Bradley Wellington for contributing "Tech Talk"
Design by Lynne Amft

Produced by 17th Street Productions,
an Alloy Online, Inc. company
33 West 17th Street, New York, NY 10011

Library of Congress Cataloging-in-Publication Data

Sherman, Josepha.
Jeff Bezos : king of amazon.com / by Josepha Sherman.
p. cm. — (Techies)
Includes index.
ISBN 0-7613-1963-8 (lib. bdg.)
1. Bezos, Jeffrey—Juvenile literature. 2. Booksellers and bookselling—United States—
Biography—Juvenile literature. 3. Amazon.com—History—Juvenile literature. 4. Internet
bookstores—United States—Juvenile literature. 5. Electronic commerce—United States—
Juvenile literature. [1. Bezos, Jeffrey. 2. Booksellers and bookselling. 3. Businesspeople. 4.
Amazon.com.] I. Title. II. Series.
Z473.B47 S48   2001
380.1'45002'02854678—dc21   00-057709
[B]

lib: 10 9 8 7 6 5 4 3 2 1

contents

CHAPTER ONE

Driven by Curiosity

An Ingenious and Creative Child

WHEN JEFFREY PRESTON BEZOS—OR JEFF, AS HE PREFERS TO BE CALLED—WAS BORN IN ALBUQUERQUE, NEW MEXICO, ON JANUARY 12, 1964, THERE WERE NO SUCH THINGS AS PERSONAL COMPUTERS. THERE WAS NO INTERNET, NOR ANY WORLD WIDE WEB. NO ONE IN 1964 HAD EVEN DREAMED THAT PEOPLE MIGHT SOMEDAY BE ABLE TO BUY AND SELL THINGS OVER AN ELECTRONIC NETWORK. ALL THAT WAS YET TO COME.

HIS MOTHER, JACKIE GISE, WAS ONLY SEVENTEEN WHEN SHE GAVE BIRTH TO HER SON, BUT SHE QUICKLY ADAPTED TO

Jeff with his mom, Jackie

motherhood. Bezos (pronounced Bay-zos) never knew his natural father because his parents' marriage broke up after only a year.

It wasn't long, however, before Bezos had a father who encouraged and loved him. His new father, Michael "Mike" Bezos, had grown up in Cuba under Fidel Castro's Communist rule. He escaped to the United States when he was only fifteen. All alone in a new country, Mike Bezos was determined to succeed. Quickly learning English, he took whatever jobs he could find. By the time he was old enough to go to college, he had started working at night so that he could attend the University of New Mexico during the day.

One night while working at a bank, Mike Bezos met Jackie Gise, who was also working the night shift. The two began dating. Not long after that they fell in love. And not long after that, they married, and young Jeff had a new father, Mike Bezos. Jeff was so little that Mike immediately became Dad to him.

Later, when Jeff Bezos was ten years old, his parents told him the whole story of his birth and the fact that Mike Bezos was really his stepfather. Jeff didn't care. He thought of Mike Bezos as his real father. And he still does.

From the time he was a toddler, Bezos was busy trying to change his world. He felt he was too old to sleep in a "baby" crib, so he found a screwdriver and took the crib apart! Instead of getting mad, Bezos's family encouraged him. His grandfather, Lawrence Gise, a rancher who was retired from the Atomic Energy Commission, recognized the boy's creativity and ingenuity. Gise knew his grandson loved working on models, so Gise bought him an electronics kit. Bezos loved it. In fact, when his younger sister and brother, Christina and Mark, started toddling around the house, Bezos rigged up an alarm for his bedroom door. If Mark or Christina wandered into his room, a buzzer rang. Bezos never had to worry that they would get into his stuff without his knowing it.

When he was twelve, Bezos desperately wanted a new device called the Infinity Cube. The Infinity Cube was a set of small motorized mirrors that reflected off one another to make you feel like you were looking into infinity. Bezos was fascinated. But when his mother found out that it cost twenty dollars, she told Bezos it was just too expensive. This didn't stop Bezos. He bought the mirrors and other parts for an

Infinity Cube cheaply. He didn't have any instructions to follow, so he made his own by simply looking closely at an Infinity Cube.

Bezos invented other devices, and his experiments soon overflowed his room. They started to take up space all over the house. Finding bits of robots lying on the living-room floor was just too much for his parents. They banished his experiments to the family garage. That became his laboratory. On any day, a visitor to the garage could find half-finished bodies of robots or parts of an old vacuum cleaner that were being converted into a hovercraft.

Bezos wasn't a mad scientist who hid in his garage from other people. He had a good sense of humor and loved to laugh and be silly. He liked people and made friends easily. His people skills helped him adapt when his family began moving around. By the time Bezos was a teenager, Mike Bezos had found a good job as a petroleum engineer with Exxon. This job took the family from New Mexico to Texas, then on to Florida.

The Bezos family stayed in Florida long enough for Jeff Bezos to attend and graduate from Palmetto High School in

Thomas Edison, a hero to inventors everywhere

Miami. He did so well in high school and made so many friends that he was named valedictorian and class president.

The traveling didn't stop Bezos from learning everything he could, from science to science fiction. He particularly loved everything to do with *Star Trek* and still does. Bezos even owns a dog he named Kamala after a minor *Star Trek* character. Watching *Star Trek* kindled his interest in space science, and Bezos began to dream of becoming an astronaut. He loved the idea of building something new or traveling to a place never seen before. Inventor Thomas Edison and Walt Disney were his two favorite heroes. Bezos didn't like Walt Disney because of Mickey Mouse or Disney's movies– Bezos was amazed at how Disney used electronics to create the rides and characters he had seen at Disney World.

Every summer Bezos left the realm of science and invention to visit his grandfather's ranch in Texas. There the boy rode horses, branded cattle, and helped with the ranch work. Occasionally he would use his skills to fix a machine. He enjoyed it all, even though it was very different from his life at home. "You have to have a lot of patience," Bezos said, "on a ranch in the middle of nowhere."

Bezos on his grandfather's ranch

Jeff Bezos wasn't destined to be a rancher—everyone in his family was sure he was going to be a scientist. He was fascinated by everything to do with physics, electronics, and space. Bezos decided to go to Princeton University to study physics, determined to follow in the footsteps of another of his heroes, the famous physicist Stephen Hawking.

Once at Princeton, Bezos started to feel uncomfortable in his physics classes. All the other physics students seemed so much smarter than he was. He felt he was the only one who wouldn't succeed.

So Bezos quickly changed from physics to a double major in electronics and computer science. The first personal computer, the Altair 8800, had been invented in 1975, and by the early 1980s a young genius named Bill Gates was leading a fast-growing computer software company known as Microsoft. Bezos was one of the first students to study computer science at Princeton.

Bezos found his niche in computer science. He could create and build using computer languages. He settled down and directed his creativity and energy to his new fields. His hard work paid off in 1986, when he graduated from Princeton summa cum laude (highest honors), Phi Beta Kappa, earning degrees in electrical engineering and computer science. With such prestigious academic honors, it's difficult to imagine that Bezos wouldn't have succeeded in physics as well.

Now what? Several large corporations offered him jobs even before he graduated, but Bezos wasn't sure he wanted to work for a big company. He knew he wanted to work with computers, but he wanted to build something that had never been done before. Bezos summed up his philosophy as, "Work hard, have fun, make history."

He thought he'd found the right job when he took a position with a new company called Fitel. Fitel had been founded with a specific goal in mind: building a computer network that could handle all the complicated information and news of the world of international finance.

Bezos thought Fitel would be ideal for him. He was very good at working with computer codes, the "languages" that tell computers what to do, and he liked the idea of building a

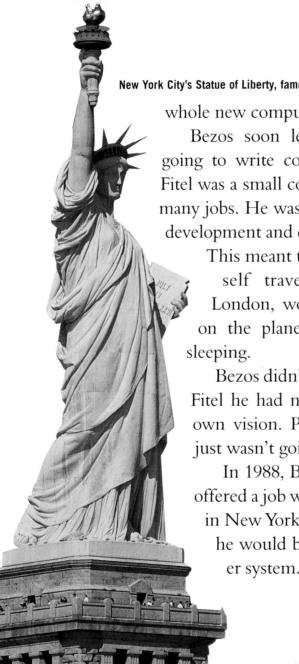

New York City's Statue of Liberty, famous beacon for dreamers

whole new computer network.

Bezos soon learned that he wasn't just going to write computer programs. Because Fitel was a small company, Bezos had to juggle many jobs. He was also expected to be head of development and director of customer service.

This meant that Bezos often found himself traveling back and forth to London, working out Fitel's problems on the plane while other people were sleeping.

Bezos didn't mind working hard. But at Fitel he had no control over building his own vision. Plus Fitel wasn't growing–it just wasn't going to succeed.

In 1988, Bezos left Fitel. He had been offered a job with Bankers Trust Company in New York City. As a product manager, he would be developing their computer system. Although Bezos was able to use his skills, it still wasn't quite what he wanted to do with his life. He still dreamed of building something radically new. Bezos worked so hard at Bankers Trust that by 1990, at age twenty-six, he made company history: He became their youngest vice president ever.

After two years at Bankers Trust, Bezos grew tired of the financial world–he knew that he didn't belong there. He wanted to work with a company that would let him use computers and new technology.

In 1990, Bezos found that company. He was hired by D. E. Shaw & Company. This was another New York financial firm–but one that believed in picking the smartest people they could find, then figuring out what they could do the best. David Shaw, the head of the company, was a computer guru just like Bezos, and the two clicked immediately. In 1992, at age twenty-eight, Bezos became D. E. Shaw's youngest vice president. By 1994 he had become a senior vice president.

Meanwhile, though, Bezos was beginning to worry about his private life. Business was taking up so much of his time, he feared he was turning into an old businessman who was married to his office. Was he ever going to meet a woman he could love and who could love him? Would he ever get married? Bezos was sure he wasn't the sort of man that women dreamed about. He had that wild, silly sense of humor and loved to laugh. Dashing and romantic hardly–he thought of himself as "kind of goofy." Didn't women prefer the handsome hero to the computer nerd?

Not all women. Bezos met a young woman who worked right in the same office. They'd both been working at D. E. Shaw for two years, yet they had never met. Her name was MacKenzie Tuttle, and she was a research associate and a budding novelist. As they got to know each other better, they learned that they'd both attended Princeton. They had never met there, either. Their paths had finally crossed.

She and Bezos started dating and fell in love. They got married in 1992.

CHAPTER TWO

Taking a Risk

Awaking to the Internet Invasion

HAPPILY MARRIED, BEZOS MIGHT HAVE GONE RIGHT ON WORKING WITH D. E. SHAW AND STAYED IN THE WORLD OF HIGH FINANCE IF IT HADN'T BEEN FOR THE INTERNET. HE WAS FASCINATED BY THIS ELECTRONIC NETWORK THAT COULD LINK COMPUTERS AROUND THE WORLD. HE SPENT HOURS EXPLORING IT.

THE INTERNET HAD STARTED AS AN ELECTRONIC SYSTEM CALLED ARPANET. IT HAD BEEN CREATED TO HELP THE U.S. MILITARY AROUND THE WORLD KEEP IN TOUCH. BUT

ARPANET quickly grew and changed, spreading into a network of university computers. Now it had become the Internet, growing into a whole world in itself. The U.S. government agreed that it couldn't claim to own the whole Internet and would allow private companies to use it as well.

One day in May 1994, while Bezos was exploring the Internet, he stumbled on a site that claimed to measure Internet usage. Bezos read the figures, then read them again. He couldn't believe what he was seeing. According to this site, the Internet was growing at over 2,300 percent a year!

"It was a wake-up call," Bezos said.

He started thinking about this right away. His mind whirled with ideas. Here was a perfect chance for a business to use the new technology to reach a new, constantly growing market. But what kind of business? What kind of business could be run on the Internet better than it could in the everyday world?

Bezos began doing his homework. First he looked at mail-order companies. After all, those were companies that successfully sold products by mail rather than in stores. Wouldn't they work just as well selling those products on the Internet?

Bezos read hundreds of mail-order catalogs and studied hundreds of mail-order companies. He made a list of the top-twenty mail-order companies. What were they selling? What did they have in common? And what could be sold online that would be easy for a customer to buy, easier than buying it in a store?

Then the big idea struck him. Books! There weren't any complete mail-order catalogs for books because there were just too many books–more than three million different titles available in print worldwide each year. And new titles were published every month. There were also more types of books, from fiction to textbooks, than any one mail-order company could handle. But the Internet had room for endless amounts of information–it could hold all of the types and all of the titles.

Bezos couldn't go any further with this idea yet. He knew nothing about the bookselling business. But he could learn. And he knew just where to look: He started searching the Internet.

To his delight, Bezos found that an enormous conference for booksellers' business was taking place the very next day.

TECH TALK

How the Internet Works

Have you ever wondered how the Internet works? How can so much information be sent across tiny wires and always arrive at the correct place? This is all achieved through the use of "packets." A packet is a bundle of information that one computer sends to another. You can think of a packet like you would think of an envelope at a post office. There is some information inside, but unless it's yours, you see only the address and the return address. The part of the packet that's like the front of the envelope is called the packet's header. The header contains information about the sender of the packet as well as where the packet is going. Every computer on the Internet receives many packets every day. In fact, there are special machines that are meant just to receive packets. These machines are called routers. They look at the packets coming in, and if they aren't for them, they forward them in the right direction. No matter how far a packet has to go, even if it has to stop at a hundred places, it will always get to where it's going because it will always be forwarded in the right direction.

The inside of a packet can contain any kind of information—e-mail, Web pages, instant messages, files, music, and even video. But because a package is small, something large (like a video) must be broken up and sent in several different packets. The computer that receives these packets then puts them together.

This was the American Booksellers Association yearly event, the ABA conference, which is held in a different city each year. In 1994 it was being held in Los Angeles.

Bezos caught a plane and flew to Los Angeles the next day. He spent the whole weekend wandering the conference aisles and attending meetings, absorbing as much knowledge as he possibly could about the bookselling business. There was almost too much information for one person to digest in so short a time—but everything he saw and heard made Bezos feel that he was on the right track.

He quickly realized that he'd been correct. No one bookstore, not even one of the enormous superstores, could keep a complete list of every book in print. Bezos learned that there were distribution companies such as Ingram and Baker & Taylor. These large distributors specialized in actually getting books to the bookstores. He spoke to the people at Ingram and at Baker & Taylor and discovered that both companies had recently moved their books-in-print lists onto the Internet so that there would be enough room to list all the books that were being published.

A Big Decision

This information was just what he'd been hoping to hear. Bezos hurried back to D. E. Shaw, full of excitement about the idea of selling books over the Internet. He couldn't wait to share what he had learned.

The response he got surprised him. To his disappointment, no one there was interested in starting an online bookselling business. It sounded too risky, and no one knew how long the Internet would stay popular. Now Bezos was faced with a very difficult decision. Could he just drop the idea of selling books over the Internet? No, he didn't want to let that go. He had finally found a way to use his computer and business skills to create something totally new.

Still, he had a good job at D. E. Shaw, one where he was very happy. Did he dare to leave it? Bezos talked the whole thing over with his wife.

MacKenzie Bezos was almost as excited about the Internet and its growth as her husband, and she wasn't afraid of making a major change in their lives. Bezos warned her that most of the new Internet companies failed and only about one in ten

Internet companies stayed in business for more than a year.

Together they decided they were willing to take the risk.

Bezos went to David Shaw and resigned. Shaw took him for a long walk in New York's Central Park, trying to convince him to stay and insisting that Bezos at least take two days to think it over.

He did just that, and the decision grew more difficult. What was he going to do? How could he choose? Finally Bezos asked himself, "When I'm eighty, am I going to regret leaving Wall Street?"

No, he decided, he wouldn't regret that at all.

"Will I regret missing a chance to be there at the beginning of the Internet?"

Yes. He would.

That was it. He had just made his decision.

Bezos's family was uneasy when they heard his decision. Mike Bezos couldn't believe that his son wanted to leave a safe, well-paying job. He also couldn't believe that the reason Bezos was leaving was to start up a new company. Didn't his son realize how risky this was? And an Internet company was even more risky! There was at best, he told his son, only a 30 percent chance of success. Mike Bezos wasn't even sure that the Internet itself was going to be around for very long.

But Jeff Bezos was determined. So Mike and Jackie Bezos finally agreed to help finance their son's idea. They didn't believe in the new company or the Internet. As Jackie Bezos summed it up, "We invested in Jeff."

Bezos resigned from D. E. Shaw. He and his wife packed

Seattle, Washington, hotbed of high tech

up all their belongings and started the drive across the country to Seattle, Washington. They chose Seattle because it was the home of Ingram's main West Coast warehouses. Being so close to the warehouses of one of the biggest book distributors would make it much easier and cheaper to fill book orders.

Seattle was also the home of Bill Gates's enormous software company, Microsoft. Microsoft drew programmers and computer whizzes to the area, just the type of people Bezos needed to start his company.

From Abracadabra to Amazon

On the way to Seattle, Bezos designed a business plan, typing it out on his laptop computer while his wife drove. To him, creating the plan for the company was the easy part. Coming up with a name to call his new company was unexpectedly hard. He just couldn't decide. He wanted something powerful but catchy, something that would last forever.

"What about Abracadabra?" Bezos asked his wife.

Abracadabra is a word that stage magicians often use.

Bezos liked the idea of an Internet company being compared to something magical. But MacKenzie Bezos shook her head. She thought that Abracadabra was just too long for an online name and too difficult for people to spell.

"What about shortening it to just Cadabra?" Bezos asked a lawyer.

The lawyer didn't hear him clearly. "Cadaver?" he asked in confusion.

The lawyer had thought Bezos wanted to name his company after a dead body. Cadabra was clearly not going to work as a company name.

Then Bezos had a sudden inspiration. What about calling the company Amazon? The name

The mighty Amazon River

started with A, which put it at the front of an alphabetical search, and it was short and easy to spell. Besides, Amazon was powerful and eternal. After all, the Amazon River, the world's longest river, flowed through Brazil in South America for mile after mile, seemingly forever. Bezos hoped his online business would flow on and on forever, too. "It's Earth's biggest river, Earth's biggest bookstore," he decided.

Of course, some people would think that he had named his company after the warrior women of Greek mythology, the Amazons. But that wasn't so bad, either. After all, the Amazons were strong and triumphed over all sorts of hardships.

Amazon was it, then. Most companies have to add a ".com" to their online addresses since that's the code that lets computers locate them, so Amazon.com would be Bezos's new company's official name.

In Search of Electricity and Employees

Now that the company had a name, it was time to find it a home. One advantage of selling over the Internet, Bezos knew, was that he didn't need an expensive office. An Internet business can be run from anywhere if there's a computer and a modem to connect the computer to the Internet. Jeff and MacKenzie Bezos rented a two-bedroom house in Bellevue, a Seattle suburb. This would be the new headquarters for Amazon.com.

They turned the house's small garage into the Amazon work area and set up three linked computer systems. Bezos was back to a garage laboratory, this time to create a company. There wasn't much room. Computer cables snaked across the floor in all directions, and Bezos and his wife were always tripping over wires.

Now there was another problem. Did they have enough electricity to run everything? When he first tried turning on all the systems, Bezos blew a fuse. He kept on blowing fuses every time he added a new computer. There just wasn't enough electrical power available in the garage.

Bezos began drawing in electricity from the house itself. Now there were big orange power cables adding to the tangle of wires in the garage. Of course, this meant that there was less electricity in their home. By now neither Bezos nor his wife dared run even a vacuum cleaner in their house, or they'd black out the whole company.

To save money, Bezos built office furniture, desks, and bookcases alike, out of old doors and pieces of lumber, hammering everything together as best as he could. As Bezos put it frankly, "These weren't very attractive offices."

MacKenzie Bezos eagerly helped her husband to get Amazon.com up and running, and she assumed whatever role was needed. She took on a part-time job as the new company's accountant. She also helped interview people who wanted to work for Amazon. Since there really wasn't enough room in the garage for interviews, the couple often held their meetings with would-be employees in the local coffee shop. Later on, Bezos looked back at those meetings and laughed. That coffee shop belonged to what was going to become Amazon's main rival–the bookstore chain called Barnes & Noble.

The first person Bezos hired was Shel Kaphan. He turned out to be one of the most important employees of Amazon. com. Kaphan was an expert computer programmer.

But Kaphan had joined several young Internet companies only to be frustrated when many of them failed. When Bezos contacted him, Kaphan had just left Kaleida Labs, a spin-off company from Apple Computer that had just failed. By this time Kaphan really didn't know if he wanted to risk working with another new Internet company. It took Bezos several months of coaxing to convince Kaphan to leave California and move north to Amazon's garage headquarters in Seattle.

Bezos didn't tell Kaphan just how makeshift the Amazon office was. He stopped himself just in time from asking, "How big a door do you need for your desk? And how tall do you want me to build it?" Knowing how small Amazon.com really was would have scared Kaphan away!

Once Kaphan was actually at Amazon.com, he must have been startled by what he saw. But he didn't quit. As he worked, though, he kept muttering about how often companies failed. Bezos soon realized that was just the way Kaphan was. Even while the man was prophesying failure, he kept right on dealing with the computers, making Amazon.com succeed.

The next person Bezos hired was a contractor named Paul Barton-Davis. By now the garage was so crowded with computers and computer cables that many of Bezos's meetings with Barton-Davis were held in Barnes & Noble's coffee shop as well.

Bezos was very, very careful about the people he hired. He insisted on going over every detail of the would-be employee's abilities. He would ask question after question. If the potential employee made the slightest mistake or wouldn't answer a question about former employment, Bezos wouldn't hire him or her. Bezos wasn't being mean, just careful. He knew that with such a new, small company, there just wasn't room or money for anyone who wouldn't be useful. Every employee had to contribute to make Amazon better and stronger.

CHAPTER THREE

"Work Hard, Have Fun, Make History"

Open for Business

Next Bezos had to find money to pay his employees and get the company started. The $300,000 that Bezos had gotten from his parents might have seemed like a lot of money, but it wasn't really very much for supporting a new business. Amazon needed to raise more money as quickly as possible.

This was Bezos's job. He liked dealing with people. Speaking eagerly and persuasively, he quickly managed to convince fifteen investors to put money into Amazon.com. Some of these investors were people from New York who he'd known when he had worked for Bankers Trust or D. E. Shaw. Others were friends of the family. He also interested a group of Seattle investors who believed in his vision.

Now Amazon.com had the money it needed–a million dollars. It was ready to be launched on the Internet.

The first version of the Amazon.com Web site was created in June 1995 and posted at a temporary, secret Web address, HYPERLINK "http://www.amazon.com:99." That address no longer exists. It was there just to give Bezos a chance to have beta testers check over the Web site for errors.

A beta tester is someone who enjoys testing an Internet site or computer program while it's still in its beginning, or beta, stage. Bezos invited no fewer than three hundred beta testers to try out his new site and see if it was stable. The three hundred did everything they could to make the site crash or fail. But it didn't crash. To Bezos's delight, Amazon.com's Web site proved to be every bit as stable as he'd hoped. The site was ready for the world.

TECH TALK

Internet Protocol IP Addresses

Have you ever wondered why every Web page starts with "http://"? That stands for hypertext transfer protocol. A protocol is a language, just like English or French. It's the language computers use to communicate with one another. Every time something is sent over the Internet, it's sent in its own special language.

Hypertext transfer protocol is the protocol for Web pages. It contains not only text but "tags" and also things like links to other pages and graphics. Some other protocols are ftp://, for file transfer protocol (used for downloads) and "smtp," for simple mail transfer protocol (used for e-mail).

On July 6, 1995, Amazon.com officially opened for business.

Bezos and his staff knew that the very first orders would come from family and friends. They couldn't get very excited about that.

But on July 16 the first unknown customer placed an order, for a science book titled *Fluid Concepts and Creative Analogies: Computer Models of the Fundamental Mechanisms of Thought*, by Douglas R. Hofstadter. Everyone at Amazon.com got excited when they didn't recognize the customer's name. Cries of, "Do you know him?" "No, do you?" ran through the garage. Thrilled, they realized that he was a complete stranger. He had come to buy a book on his own. This was Amazon.com's first real customer!

That was only the beginning. Bezos and Kaphan had rigged up a system on the computers that would ring like a bell every time someone ordered a book. After a few days they had to disconnect the bell because the constant ringing was driving everyone in the garage crazy.

In less than a month, with almost no publicity, Bezos found that he had sold books in all fifty states. He'd even sold books in forty-five other countries.

"Within the first few days, I knew this was going to be huge," Bezos said. "It was obvious that we were on to something much bigger than we ever dared to hope."

As Amazon was getting started, another Internet company, Yahoo.com, was beginning to establish itself, too. Yahoo.com wasn't interested in selling anything. It was a search engine, which is an online site that helps people find what they're hunting for on the Internet.

Bezos received a message from the people at Yahoo.com. They really liked the look of Amazon.com, and they wanted to list it in their "What's Cool" section. That pleased Bezos. But he didn't realize just how big and important Yahoo.com was going to become.

He also didn't realize that a lot of people had already started checking out the "What's Cool" section every day. When they read Amazon's new listing in "What's Cool", many of them went straight from there to Amazon.com and became customers.

Something else helped Amazon–the fact that Bezos thought long and hard about customers. Of course, every

TECH TALK

Search Engines

Have you ever used a search engine on the World Wide Web to find something? How does it keep track of all the Web pages out there? How does it know when someone writes their home page? In order to accomplish the enormous task of looking at every page on every site on the Web, developers came up with what is called a Web crawler. This is a computer program written to look only at Web pages. It will look at a page, find the title and so on, save that, and then go to all the links to that page and do the same thing. The crawler can find millions of pages very quickly.

Let's say you have a page with ten links to other pages. And each of those pages has links to ten pages. And each of those pages has links to ten pages.

You have just found a thousand pages, starting with just one. Many search engines that use crawlers leave them constantly running because they almost never run out of possible Web pages to look at.

smart businessperson believes in making customers happy. But Bezos knew that making them happy was even more important for an online business. When shopping at an online store, there couldn't be any face-to-face contact with another human being. A customer could easily do comparison shopping online, checking the price for the same product on different sites without moving from the computer. And if the customer wasn't happy with what was on a site, he or she could leave with just a click of a mouse.

Bezos told the Amazon staff that they had to devote most of their time and energy to creating a good experience for the book buyer—and stressing the importance of that seemed to work. Amazon welcomed many new customers and more and more repeat ones.

Amazon.com grew so quickly that Bezos found himself faced with aspects of business that he had never thought of before. Online images are called virtual, meaning that they're things that can't actually be touched. The book orders that people were placing through Amazon.com were virtual. But the books themselves were very real. Now stacks of books were piled in between the tangled computer wires and employees. The garage had been small even when business was mainly virtual.

Bezos was so overwhelmed by the suddenness of the company's growth that he didn't always see the most obvious solution to a problem. To pack up book orders, for instance, Bezos and his employees had to crouch or kneel on the garage floor. That was tiring and hard on the knees. Bezos wondered aloud if he should buy everyone knee pads to protect their knees. An employee pointed out that what they needed to buy was a packing table so they didn't have to kneel at all!

Outgrowing the Garage

It wasn't long before Amazon.com had grown so fast and so large that it had outgrown that one crowded garage. The business now needed its own warehouse, and Bezos found one not too far away.

The warehouse wasn't too much bigger than the garage, and it had only a six-foot ceiling. One worker who was over six feet tall had to stoop whenever he was in there. But even a small warehouse was a big help. Now orders could be shipped out to customers in far less time. A warehouse also gave Bezos's employees the chance to quickly combine orders for books from more than one publisher.

Bezos remembers that time very clearly. It was downright hectic. Everyone at Amazon.com took turns packing books, sometimes staying up till two or three in the morning to finish the orders. No one could fall asleep on the job because there just wasn't the time–or the room.

One of the employees took a moment to look over this frantic little distribution center in the middle of a small warehouse with a low ceiling. He shook his head and said, "This is either incredibly optimistic or hopelessly pathetic."

The right word did seem to be optimistic. Even with the lack of space and time, there was no doubt that Amazon.com was working.

This young Internet company that was showing signs of success in so short a time began attracting attention. The name Amazon became familiar wherever people were online. But it also began to fascinate people in the world of big business and high finance.

In May 1996, the important business newspaper *The Wall Street Journal* ran a story on the front page about Amazon.com and Jeff Bezos. This was a sign to the world that Amazon.com was a success. All the newspaper's readers read about Amazon, and many of them flocked to the site as new customers.

Competing with "Brick-and-Mortar"

Someone else read that *Wall Street Journal* article. But unlike those new customers, he wasn't at all happy about Amazon.com or Jeff Bezos. The man was Leonard Riggio, chairman of the board of the giant national chain of bookstores Barnes & Noble. Studying the article, he realized that Amazon.com was no longer just another Internet start-up company. He couldn't ignore it. It wasn't going to fail. Barnes & Noble suddenly and unexpectedly had a major competitor.

What could they do? Barnes & Noble scrambled to meet its new opponent. But designing its own bookselling Web site would take over a year. In the meantime Barnes & Noble wanted to find a way to stop Amazon. But Jeff Bezos wasn't making

A brick-and-mortar branch of Barnes & Noble, the bookselling giant and Amazon's rival

any mistakes, and he had a financial advantage. He had lower operating expenses. That meant he didn't spend as much on running his business. Barnes & Noble had to spend millions of dollars a year building and running its "brick-and-mortar" stores. Amazon escaped all the usual costs of a bookseller. It didn't have to operate any outside stores. It didn't have to pay salespeople. It didn't have to keep massive amounts of inventory. Amazon.com didn't have any building costs at all.

Because of the money saved, Bezos could afford to offer customers a discount on every book they bought through Amazon. Some investors in Amazon.com were a little worried about this. Didn't a discount mean that Amazon.com would lose money on every book? No, Bezos explained, it didn't. All professional booksellers buy books at a specific discount. So Amazon could afford to pass on to customers a piece of that discount.

By the middle of 1996 the Barnes & Noble site, called Barnesandnoble.com, was almost ready to be launched on the Internet. Jeff Bezos wasn't worried–at least not in public. Amazon.com was already taking the next step for a new and successful company. It was "going public." This meant that

Bezos was offering to sell shares of Amazon.com stock–allowing the public to own small pieces of the company.

When a company sells a share of stock, the person who buys the share is gambling that the company will be more profitable and more valuable in the future. Every time someone buys a share, the cost of every share goes up.

The names of all companies listed on a stock market are abbreviated for convenience. Amazon.com's abbreviated name turned out to be AMZN. This looked like Amazon–it also looked like amazing. A word that perfectly described the company's immediate success.

But Amazon's stock wasn't so amazing at first. It sold for only eighteen dollars a share. This actually wasn't a very high price for shares in a successful company. What was wrong?

It turned out that the important financial analysts still weren't sure that Amazon was going to be a lasting success. They were worried about the competition from Barnes & Noble–particularly since they knew Barnes & Noble was just about to open its own bookselling Web site. *Fortune* magazine even ran an article titled, "Why Barnes & Noble May Crush Amazon.com."

The Battle Turns Legal

In May 1997, Barnes & Noble finally launched its Web site. At the same time, on almost the same day that the site opened for business, Barnes & Noble brought a lawsuit against Amazon. Amazon.com, they said, claimed that it was "the world's largest bookstore." The suit argued that since Amazon.com wasn't an actual brick-and-mortar bookstore, it couldn't call itself "the largest." The suit claimed Amazon was using false advertising.

Bezos prepared to fight back with a lawsuit of his own. Internet stores don't have to pay state taxes except in the state in which they're based since they don't have any physical stores. Amazon promptly issued a countersuit that claimed that if Barnes & Noble was going to sell books online while it owned brick-and-mortar stores, it should pay state taxes whenever customers buying books from Barnesandnoble.com lived in those states where Barnes & Noble had stores.

In October 1997, rather than fight what would have been a long and expensive lawsuit, Amazon.com and Barnes & Noble settled the matter out of court. The people studying the case afterward agreed that even though it had never gone to court and no one had gotten any money from it, Amazon.com had won. Jeff Bezos had proved to the world that he wasn't afraid of a larger company. He wasn't going to surrender to anyone.

But everyone knew that the battle between the two companies was far from over.

In its first year Barnesandnoble.com lagged behind Amazon. It didn't have the friendly appearance that Amazon.com did. It wasn't as easy to use, either. What's more, Barnesandnoble.com crashed several times. It had a number of errors, such as misspellings of author names or titles, which needed to be corrected. Many of these problems were corrected in later years. But Barnesandnoble.com didn't make the splash it was hoping to.

Meanwhile Amazon.com continued to attract new customers as well as keeping the old ones. Barnes & Noble and its lawsuit hadn't slowed down Bezos's success at all.

When they realized what was happening, the financial analysts began changing their minds about Amazon. They began recommending its stock after all. People started buying shares.

The more they bought, the more money they put into the company and the more valuable Amazon.com became. The value of Amazon's stock, which had hovered around $3 for many months, shot up to $50 in 1998. By 1999 each share was worth over $100. Investors all over the world became fanatically excited about the future of etaling—the business of selling products on the web—and of all the etail companie, Amazon was the darling.

Internet companies often see their value shoot up in an amazingly short time. The owners become instantly rich. This had already happened to Bill Gates and Microsoft. Now it was happening to Jeff Bezos and Amazon.com, too. In only one year Amazon.com went from being worth under a million dollars to being worth hundreds of millions of dollars. All of a sudden Jeff Bezos found that he was a millionaire hundreds of times over! Not only that, he became one of the richest men in the world.

Did this sudden wealth change Bezos? Surprisingly, not very much. As he put it, the only real difference was that now he "didn't have to look at the prices on a menu anymore." He could order any meal he wanted.

Bezos didn't waste any of Amazon.com's money. The only expensive thing he and his wife did with their new wealth was go shopping for a house bigger than the cramped one that had been Amazon.com's headquarters. They now live in a sprawling house on the shores of Seattle's Lake Washington, not too far from the estate of that other computer millionaire, Bill Gates.

CHAPTER FOUR

A Customer-Centric Vision

Candid Feedback, Improved Service

Most of Amazon's profits went straight back into improving the company. Amazon.com still had only one small warehouse in Seattle. Bezos realized that this was one of his company's major weaknesses. What if a customer lived in New York? Books ordered in New York would have to be shipped from Seattle, in the Pacific Northwest, on the other side of the country from New York. They might not reach the New York customer for over two weeks.

Bezos knew that customers don't like to wait that long. As he has often said, "We want to be the world's most customer-centric company." Amazon.com should be, he repeated, focused directly on the customer.

So Bezos bought a second warehouse in Delaware. East Coast orders could now be shipped right from the East Coast. Now a New York customer could receive the books he or she had ordered in only a few days. Bezos bought a third warehouse in Nevada so that he could quickly ship orders to California, which has a large book-buying population.

Amazon.com did some television and radio advertising as well as running advertisements in several magazines. But Bezos knew that most of his company's business would continue to come, as it always had, from word-of-mouth recommendations.

Thanks to the Internet, word of mouth is no longer limited to face-to-face recommendations. One customer could e-mail friends all over the country or all over the world, praising Amazon.com–or complaining about it.

Bezos was well aware of how easy e-mail is to send. In fact, he used e-mail from customers as a free form of customer relations so that he didn't need to hire any expensive consultants. A customer who was happy–or unhappy–with Amazon could quickly let the company know by e-mail. Since people writing e-mail are often less careful about what they say than if they are talking face-to-face with someone or writing regular mail, the e-mail would usually be both blunt and honest. This made it very useful to Amazon.

Bezos said, "You get these very candid pieces of feedback that tell you exactly how you can improve your service."

He usually acted on these customer suggestions. Bezos also started allowing customers to review, right on the Web site pages, the books they bought from Amazon.com. This was a gamble, but a careful one. Bezos knew that some of the reviews by customers might be five-star raves, but others might be negative or even border on the cruel or just plain nasty.

This risk of negative publicity surprised and alarmed publishers. Wouldn't bad reviews hurt book sales? But Bezos argued that the chance of readers using these "real" reviews to find and enjoy a book they might not otherwise read was worth the chance of an occasional bad review.

Jeff Bezos preaches the gospel of customer service

The authors weren't left out of all this, either. Authors could post essays about any of their titles or be interviewed by Amazon.com and have their comments and interviews linked to their titles. Customers could go to one site and find reviews, articles, and the books themselves.

Bezos wasn't interested in selling only the latest best-seller. Any bookstore could do that. But all brick-and-mortar bookstores had a limit to their shelf space, so some books were always going to be left out. Amazon.com didn't have to worry about shelf space. The company could carry any book in print. This included offbeat books and books published by presses that just didn't have much of a budget for advertising. Bezos has said he feels a commitment to showcase those good books that might not normally get noticed.

A Winning Situation

Even with all the advantages of Amazon, an online company has to keep looking new and fresh to keep attracting customers. Bezos didn't forget about updating Amazon.com's

Web site frequently. He was constantly overseeing improvements. The Web site had to continue to look friendly to the new or returning customer and make someone stopping at the site for the first time want to stay for a longer visit.

Now, whenever a regular customer logged on to the site, the customer was met by name with a personalized welcome. Regular customers were offered recommendations, too, based on their tastes. At first the recommendations program didn't work as well as it could and included errors and books the customer had already bought. But Bezos upgraded the program so that customers could correct it.

Amazon used customers' book choices to attract them to new titles. Whenever a customer clicked to buy a book, a listing of other titles or authors that the reader might like as well appeared at the bottom of the page. There was even a way to look up the most popular books in a reader's hometown.

Bezos also started up the Amazon Associates program. Anyone who wanted to link his or her Web site to that of Amazon.com could do so. This meant that a visitor could, with a click of the mouse, go directly from an outside Web site to Amazon.com.

This was what Bezos called "a win, win, win" situation.

Win number one: It was a good idea for Amazon.com because it brought in new customers.

Win number two: It was good for the associates because if someone visited Amazon.com through that Web site and ordered a book, the owner of the Web site got a royalty.

Win number three: It was good for the visitor. If he or she was visiting a Web site on horses, for example, the Amazon.com page would show a list of selected books about horses.

By the end of 1999 there were over 350,000 Amazon Associates. The list included everyone from the online staff of CNet.com, a major computer news site, to Netscape, a major Internet browser, down to individual authors and small businesses, including one billing itself as "the Web's oldest and best place to buy meteorites." In December 1999, Bezos sent all of the Amazon Associates T-shirts as Christmas presents.

Meanwhile he knew that there were still people who were afraid of buying anything over the Internet for fear that someone online might steal their credit card numbers.

Bezos didn't want anyone to be afraid to shop at Amazon. So he and his programmers designed a form of "secure server" and installed it on Amazon.com. A secure server is a form of Internet security. Any private information, like a credit card number, that the customer types onto Amazon's order page is encrypted, transformed into a secure code. Now a customer could buy books using a credit card and not have to worry about hackers stealing the card's number.

Bezos was never satisfied. He was constantly hunting for ways to improve Amazon's service. When a customer sent Amazon.com a question by e-mail, Bezos made sure that the customer got an answer right away. The same was true if someone telephoned the company.

Bezos also insisted that the ordering system be improved and simplified. If a customer wanted a book sent as a gift, Amazon offered a choice of several designs of gift-wrapping paper. A book could be sent directly from Amazon.com already wrapped, with a personal gift message enclosed.

But Bezos wanted to speed up the actual ordering as well, and he knew he could use his computer science background to make more improvements. He and his computer staff invented a system for Amazon.com that they called 1-Click and filed for a patent with the U.S. Patent Office on September 28, 1999. A patent protects an invention from being used by anyone else without the inventor's permission.

Once Bezos gained his patent, number 5,960,411, it meant that Amazon.com owned 1-Click. This was a "one-click" system of ordering that was faster than anyone else's method. With it, an Amazon customer was able to place an order with a single click of a mouse button.

Bezos has created other computer inventions. He holds six other patents, including four concerning the search engines used on the Amazon.com Web site and one for the individual style of secure server used by Amazon.com. The whole point of all these patents and changes is to make it easier for customers to find and buy what they want.

"We want people to feel like they're visiting a place," Bezos said, "rather than using a software application."

Customers did like Amazon. Often when a buyer shops in an online store, the fun of shopping is missing. Sometimes it feels like there's no human on the other end of a sale. Sometimes it even feels like the Web site is intended for robots, not people. But when customers came to Amazon. com, they had the feeling that there really were human beings running things. An e-mail would be answered by a real person who would give his or her name. And real Amazon employees posted what-our-staff-is-reading reviews.

The customer approach paid off. By 1998 Amazon.com was worth more on the stock market than such brick-and-mortar companies as the large department store chains JCPenney and Sears Roebuck. More than four and a half million people from 160 countries shopped on Amazon.com that year and spent over $500 million. That made Amazon.com the top online shopping site.

Popular but Unprofitable?

Amazon.com was still spending more than they were earning. Or, as Bezos put it, "Amazon.com was actually profitable in December 1995 . . . for, oh, about one hour."

By now some people were beginning to wonder if there was something wrong with the way the company was being run. How could Amazon have so many customers, they asked, yet not show a long-lasting profit? One of the major financial magazines, *Forbes*, even gave a "yes-and-no" rating to Amazon.com in 1998. The rating said that Jeff Bezos had used technology to cause "total upheaval in the centuries-old art of bookselling." *Forbes* liked that. But the rating went on to claim that as a business, Amazon.com was far from perfect.

Was that true? Certainly Amazon's customers seemed to be happy with it. And the investors didn't seem to be afraid of continuing to buy Amazon.com stock. But it was also true that Bezos was continuing his practice of turning most of Amazon's earnings back into the company to pay for improvements rather than showing a profit.

This didn't mean that the employees of Amazon.com were unhappy or underpaid. Bezos thought too much of them for that, even though there were now about a thousand of them. He deliberately kept his own salary low since he really didn't need the money and refused to give himself bonuses the way some other owners of companies did.

Bezos liked to reward people in big and unusual ways. When Shel Kaphan reached his fourth year with the company, Bezos organized what he called a "Shelebration." This turned out to be a four-day surprise weekend in Maui, Hawaii! The guests included Kaphan and his family, Bezos and his wife, and many of the Amazon staff.

Just as Amazon.com had quickly completely outgrown its original site of a garage, then a garage and warehouse, it had outgrown four different new locations in three years.

In 1999 the company moved into a huge new site near Seattle. They're still there. This one seems to have more warehouse space than they have yet been able to fill. They finally have enough room–but Bezos's next idea could change all that.

Bezos had decided that the time was right to start expanding Amazon.com further than ever before–beyond the book market. He wanted Amazon.com to be the leader in all e-commerce, which is the term for all the buying and selling that goes on over the Internet.

CHAPTER FIVE

Online Expansion

An Electronic Shopping Center

JUST AS HE'D RESEARCHED THE BOOK BUSINESS, BEZOS NOW DID RESEARCH INTO THE MUSIC BUSINESS. BEZOS DISCOVERED THAT ABOUT 300,000 MUSIC CDS WERE PRODUCED IN THE WORLD EACH YEAR. ALMOST AS MANY MOVIE AND MUSIC VIDEOS WERE PRODUCED.

THE LARGE NUMBER OF TITLES TRIGGERED MEMORIES OF THE BEGINNINGS OF AMAZON.COM. NO ONE VIDEO OR CD STORE COULD POSSIBLY CARRY EVERY TITLE IN PRINT. BUT AMAZON.COM COULD.

Bezos demonstrates he doesn't just sell books

The idea caught on even better than Bezos had expected. In fact, Amazon.com did so well at selling these new products that it started challenging some of the successful online music- and movie-selling companies. One of the biggest of them, CDNow.com, had to join up with a rival, N2K, just to survive.

Bezos didn't stop with music or videos. He said that Amazon.com was "a one-trick pony. It's just a good trick."

The trick wasn't books or music; the trick was selling online. Bezos intended to use the very same methods to sell other products as well.

He did some more research, studying other online businesses and what they sold. Seeing how an online company like EToys.com was doing better than some brick-and-mortar toy stores, Bezos added a toys division to Amazon.com. He then included an electronics division as well.

In 1999 a new method of selling emerged on the Internet. This was known as the online auction. People with things to sell could auction them off to people who wanted to buy. Soon online auctions hosted by such companies as eBay.com had become so popular that hundreds of people were buying and selling items every day. Jeff Bezos did some more research, liked what he saw, and added an auction division to Amazon.com.

Did Bezos think that his company was going to rival eBay.com? Not really. Bezos's main interest was still in selling books. He was sure that there was enough room in the world of online auctions for at least two online auction companies. And aside from the rivalry with Barnesandnoble.com, Amazon was more interested in getting and keeping customers than crushing competitors.

But when eBay launched its Great Collections section of listings by art dealers, Bezos did some homework. He didn't want Amazon's auction site to get lost in eBay's shadow. He learned that a major art auction house, Sotheby's, was going online and made a deal with them so that Sotheby's now lists some of their auctions on Amazon.com.

Bezos saw no limit to what Amazon could sell. By now he was expanding Amazon.com into an entire online shopping center. He wanted it to be able to offer customers just about any product that could be bought over the Internet. So he added an Amazon.com computer software department, and then he added a tools-and-hardware section.

There was still more to come. Soon Amazon.com had a kitchen department, a home-living department, and a lawn-and-patio department. Bezos offered Amazon.com customers a health-and-beauty section as well.

While Amazon.com expanded by creating new departments, it also expanded by buying up some small companies. In April 1999, Bezos announced that Amazon.com had bought Alexa.com, Accept.com, and Exchange.com. Alexa.com is an online navigation service. When someone visits a site, Alexa.com provides reviews about it and suggests similar sites. Accept.com is more mysterious. All that anyone except Bezos seems to know about it is that it develops" long-term e-commerce solutions." In other words, it probably works out answers to online business problems. Exchange.com provides a database, a searchable site for used books and music CDs. In May 2000, Amazon.com bought another Internet business, Manugistics Group, another "e-business solutions" company that will help Amazon.com with orders and shipping all over the world.

Amazon.com also bought shares in several other companies

in 1999 and 2000. These ranged from Drugstore.com, an online pharmacy, to Gear.com, an online sporting goods store, to Greg Manning Auctions, an online art dealer.

The only company Bezos didn't seem to want was a book publisher. He just didn't see any point in buying one. After all, Amazon.com had never been in the business of publishing books. They provided rather than produced items, and there was no reason to change that now. Bezos said, "We're really good at exactly one thing–which is helping customers discover things that they might want to buy online. And that's enough."

Beyond Books

Did this mean that Amazon.com was losing its image of being a bookseller? Bezos didn't think so. Or at least he didn't say so. He claimed that instead of being limited to being a book or music company, Amazon.com was now, with all its choices for buyers, a "customer company."

But what about selling books to other countries? Amazon.com had been shipping books from the United States overseas since the start. In fact, Bezos estimates that about 22 percent of sales are outside the United States. Amazon.com has shipped books to over 160 countries. International shipping from the United States was expensive for the customer. So Bezos opened up two overseas branches of Amazon.com, one in Britain and the other in Germany, that lets customers in those countries order their own nations' books as well. Unfortunately, it's illegal for the British editions of books to be sold in the United States, so Amazon.com can't carry them on its main site.

Amid these massive expansions, Bezos kept a wary eye on Barnes & Noble. He knew that they wouldn't give up trying to do better than Amazon.com on the Internet. He visited the Barnesandnoble.com Web site often.

The site seemed to have had most of its problems corrected. In fact, parts of it looked very familiar to Bezos–maybe even a little too familiar, he thought. In October 1999, Amazon.com sued Barnesandnoble.com, claiming that Amazon's patented 1-Click ordering process had been illegally copied.

Barnesandnoble.com, meanwhile, claimed that Amazon.com's lawsuit was just "a desperate attempt to retaliate for our growing market share."

Amazon won the lawsuit. On December 2, 1999, Barnes & Noble was issued a temporary injunction. This meant that they had been ordered by the court to stop using, at least for now, something that did seem to be a too similar version of Amazon.com's ordering process.

Amazon won that battle, but nobody really believed the war was finally over. Surely there will be further struggles between the two companies in the future.

In addition to competition, Bezos's success brought him personal recognition. In December 1999, *Time* magazine named him their Person of the Year. He was now thirty-five, the fourth-youngest person ever to win this yearly award. He was asked if he was afraid of Barnes & Noble. He answered no. What about Microsoft and its leader, Bill Gates? Bezos admitted that "if they entered our space, I would be afraid of them." But much to Bezos's relief, Bill Gates hasn't shown any interest in entering the e-commerce business.

Changes

One new technology, though, is something that both Bezos and Gates find fascinating. That is what's being called the "e-book." This is a book in electronic form, one that can be downloaded onto a full-size computer or a handheld one.

Bezos said, "I'm a huge believer in downloadable books. It's not a question of if; it's a question of when." The technology, he believes, won't be perfected for a decade or more. But he plans to be ready for the future. He thinks that the world of selling is going to change. The strip malls, he says, will disappear because they just can't offer a customer a pleasant enough shopping experience, certainly not when compared with online convenience. He also sees the surviving brick-and-mortar stores becoming more entertaining, complete with music and performances. Bezos points out that one department store, Nordstrom, has already hired a pianist to entertain its shoppers.

The Bubble

There's time, as industry analysts like to say, and then there's Internet time. Time may prove to be Bezos's biggest challenge yet. On the Internet new "storefronts" go up every day. The number of customers grows exponentially month after month. And companies like Amazon go from being experiments in e-commerce to icons of the industry in a matter of weeks or months.

In the years 1998, 1999, and even part of 2000 the stock market fell in love with the Internet. Investors saw its stunning growth potential, and everybody wanted to buy a piece of it. Investors' fanatical enthusiasm created what on Wall Street is called a bubble—a fragile, unsustainable, massive inflation in the price of stocks. And as all bubbles will do, the Internet bubble popped. In the spring of 2000 stock prices of e-commerce companies plummeted, many by as much as 90 percent. Thankfully for Bezos, Amazon held its own as the strongest, biggest, and best-known commerce site on the Internet.

Yet Amazon has not been immune to the doubts and fears

Jeff Bezos: works hard, makes history . . . and even changes diapers

that now consume Internet investors. They fear that Amazon, like many other dot coms, will burn its way through every bit of cash it has and, without the ability to turn a profit, will go out of business. In mid-July 2000 Bezos detailed a troubled second quarter for Amazon. The company lost less money than Wall Street had expected but also sold less merchandise than Wall Street had hoped. Investors and analysts didn't like the softening sales—the stock was downgraded, sending Amazon spiraling down more than 17 percent. At around $30 a share, Amazon was valued well below its high of $113 a share just eight months before.

None of this was a surprise to Bezos, especially after some Wall Street analysts turned sour on Amazon's short-term prospects and the abrupt resignation of the company's second in command, Joseph Galli. Still, Bezos took pains to paint a picture of untold future potential. Bezos believes that the best is yet to come for Amazon, stressing that the company's newer businesses, like electronics, toys, and tools, are growing faster than the book business did in 1996 and 1997. He also insists that investors caught up in the short-term doom and gloom surrounding the e-commerce industry will miss out on the long-term gains. In the world of technology, he said, "people tend to overestimate what's going to happen in the next two years and dramatically underestimate what's going to happen in the next ten years."

Although Amazon missed its sales goals, it proved that it could sell electronics and other items besides books. "The question now becomes, how much of the $5 trillion world-wide [retail] market is addressable?" Bezos asked. Now, there's a prime statement from a guy who made a garage start-up into a corporate giant—a guy who thinks as big as the Amazon.

Jeff Bezos's life had changed dramatically since he decided to quit his job and move to Seattle, though Bezos himself hadn't changed much. He was still a man who loved to laugh and have fun. He and his wife surprised everyone in their family with a game of Lazer Tag one year for Christmas. Armed with laser guns, everyone played a wild version of capture the flag one night. Bezos discovered that his mother was a really good shot.

Bezos was also still a man who liked a challenge. In March 2000, he took on the challenge of fatherhood. MacKenzie gave birth to a little boy. The delighted parents named their son Preston Bezos. In the ensuing weeks of changing dirty diapers and waking up in the middle of the night to calm the crying baby, the father gained a whole new respect for mothers. He announced publicly that now that he knew what his mother had done for him, he wished he'd been nicer to her when he was a teenager. But it was wonderful, he told everyone, seeing MacKenzie looking so happy and watching their son in her arms.

A Promising Future

Jeff Bezos doesn't believe in showing off his wealth or his intelligence. He happily describes himself as a nerd and isn't ashamed to act silly. He still loves to laugh, too, and can usually get other people laughing as well.

MacKenzie Bezos is happy, too. Not only does she have her new son but her first novel is finished and waiting for publication. And she continues to watch out for her busy husband. Whenever he has to travel on business, she packs a daily dose of vitamins in each clean pair of socks so he won't forget to take care of himself.

As for Amazon.com, the future is unknown but promising. Who knows how big it will grow? Bezos has an idea—an ambitious idea. He foresees rewards for investors who are willing to hold on to their stock shares. He foresees a company so focused on customer service that the computer shops for the customer. His vision is Amazon-like: without limits and without fear of going where no one has gone before.

But what can you expect from a boy who grew up on *Star Trek* and the Infinity Cube?

sources and bibliography

Articles

Jeff Bezos's Keynote Speach: PC Expo, NYC, 7/6/00.

"The E-Business 25." (Cover story.) *BusinessWeek* (May 15, 1999).

"How Can Tim Koogle Stay So Cool in the Face of AOL's Assault?" (Cover story.) *BusinessWeek* (May 15, 2000).

"Q&A with Amazon.com's Jeff Bezos." *BusinessWeek* (May 31, 1999).

"Q&A with Jeff Bezos.".*BusinessWeek* (Feb 10, 2000).

Web sites

www.Time.com: 1999 Person of the year, 12/27/99.

web.zdnet.com/zdnn/stories/news/0%2C4586%2C411644%2CC00.html.

www.Amazon.com (the official site): "About Amazon.com."

www.annonline.com/interviews/970106/ This site contains an audio interview with Jeff Bezos, as well as a biography.

Photography credits

AP/WorldWide Photos, 45, 56, 75; ArchivePhotos/PictureQuest, 12; Burnett, David/Contact, 8, 13, 66; Carroll, Tom/Phototake/PictureQuest, 26; DigitalVision/PictureQuest, 16; Jangoux, Jacques/Stock Connection/PictureQuest, 28

index